GW01340113

LEMON

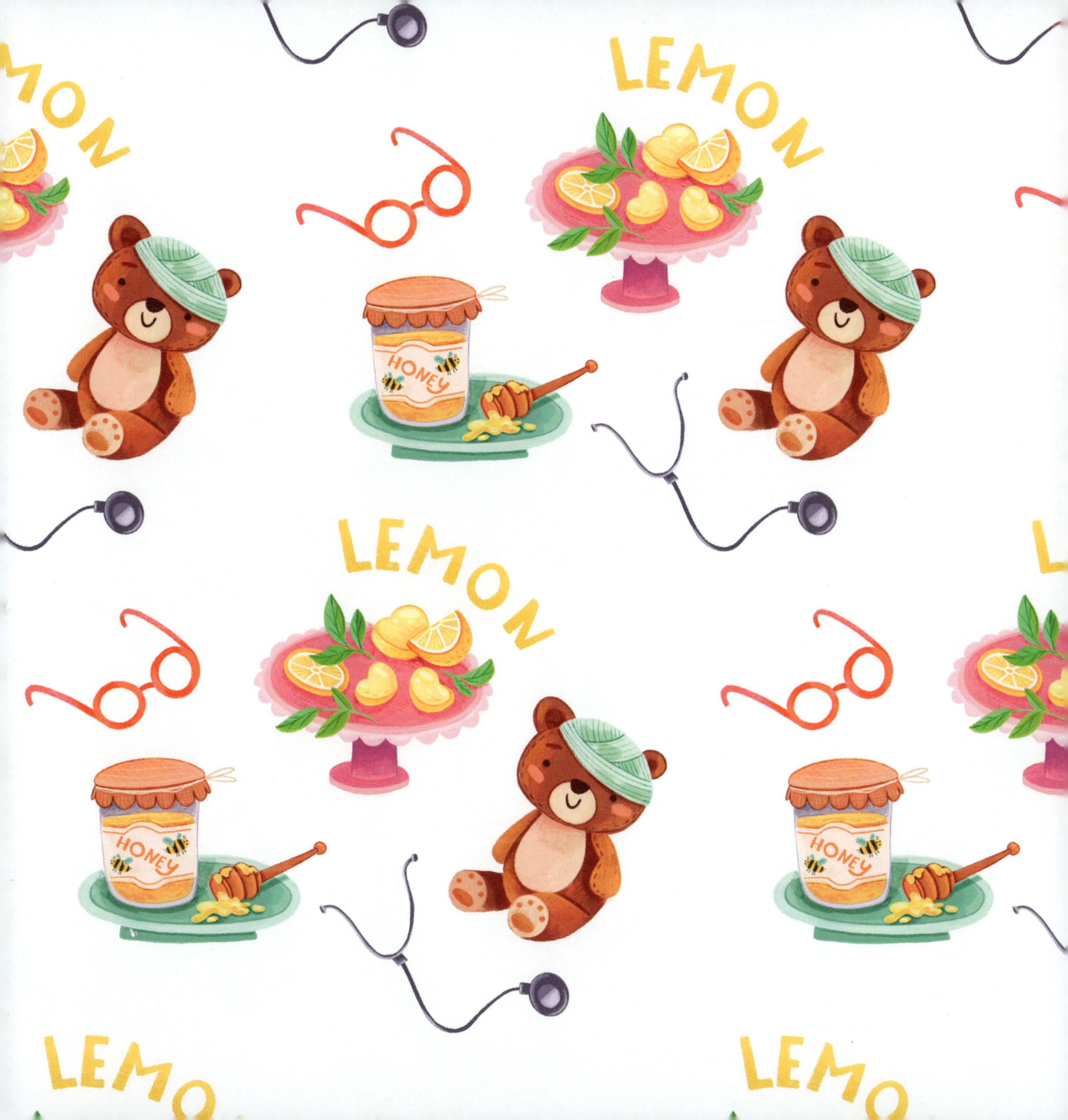
LEMON
HONEY
LEMON
HONEY
HONEY

To all the Girls and boys who want to be a doctor

I will Never Ever eat Lemon

ANA BALL

illustrated by
ANASTASIIA BIELIK

Bear loves LEMON
– it is always in his glass of water

Dolly Loves LEMON
– it is always on top of her cake

Piggy loves LEMON
– it is always in his back pocket

And even our cat Donut loves Lemon

— it is always in his paws!

But I will **NEVER EVER** eat LEMON

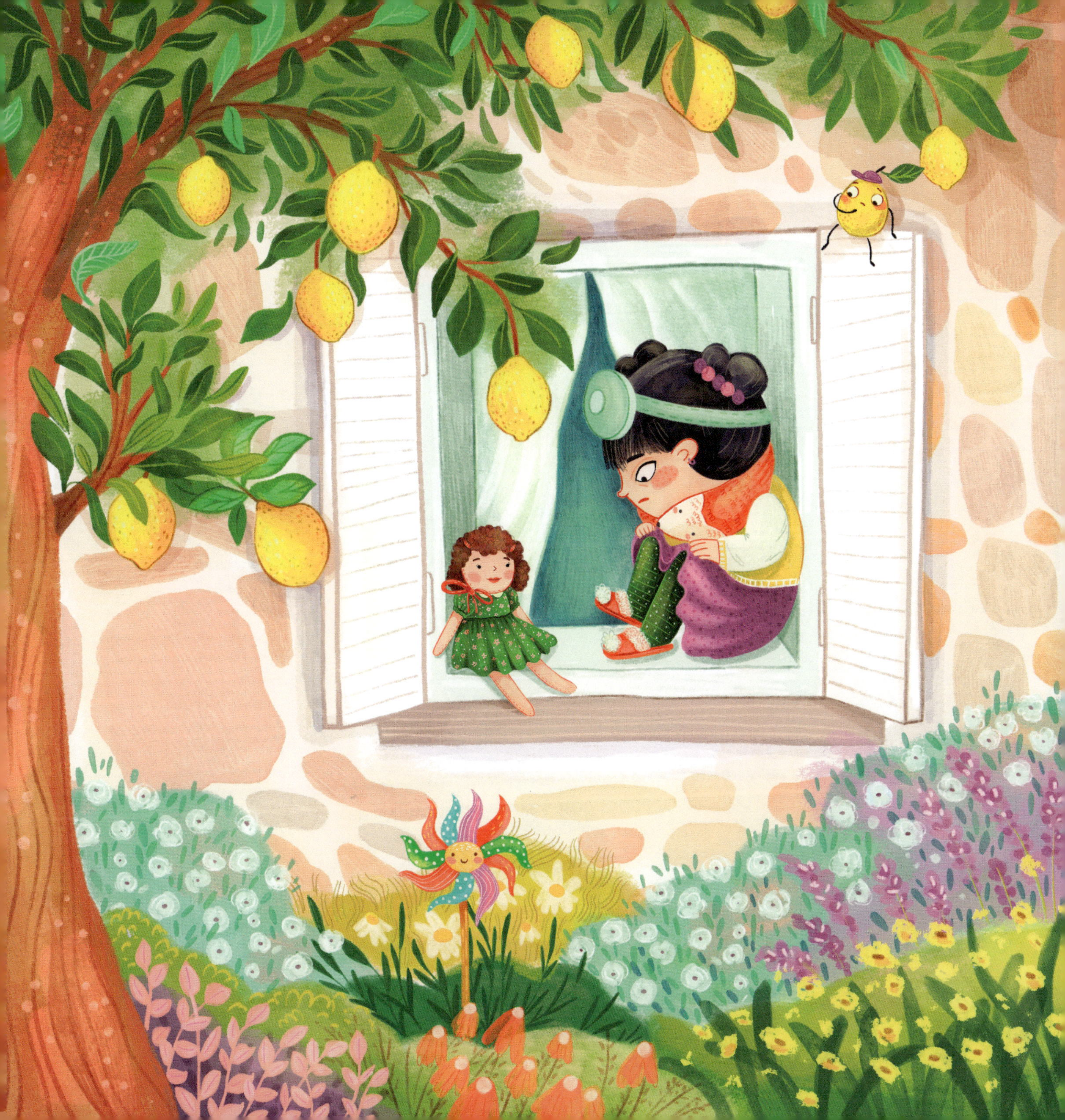

it's too YELLOW!

it's too SOUR!

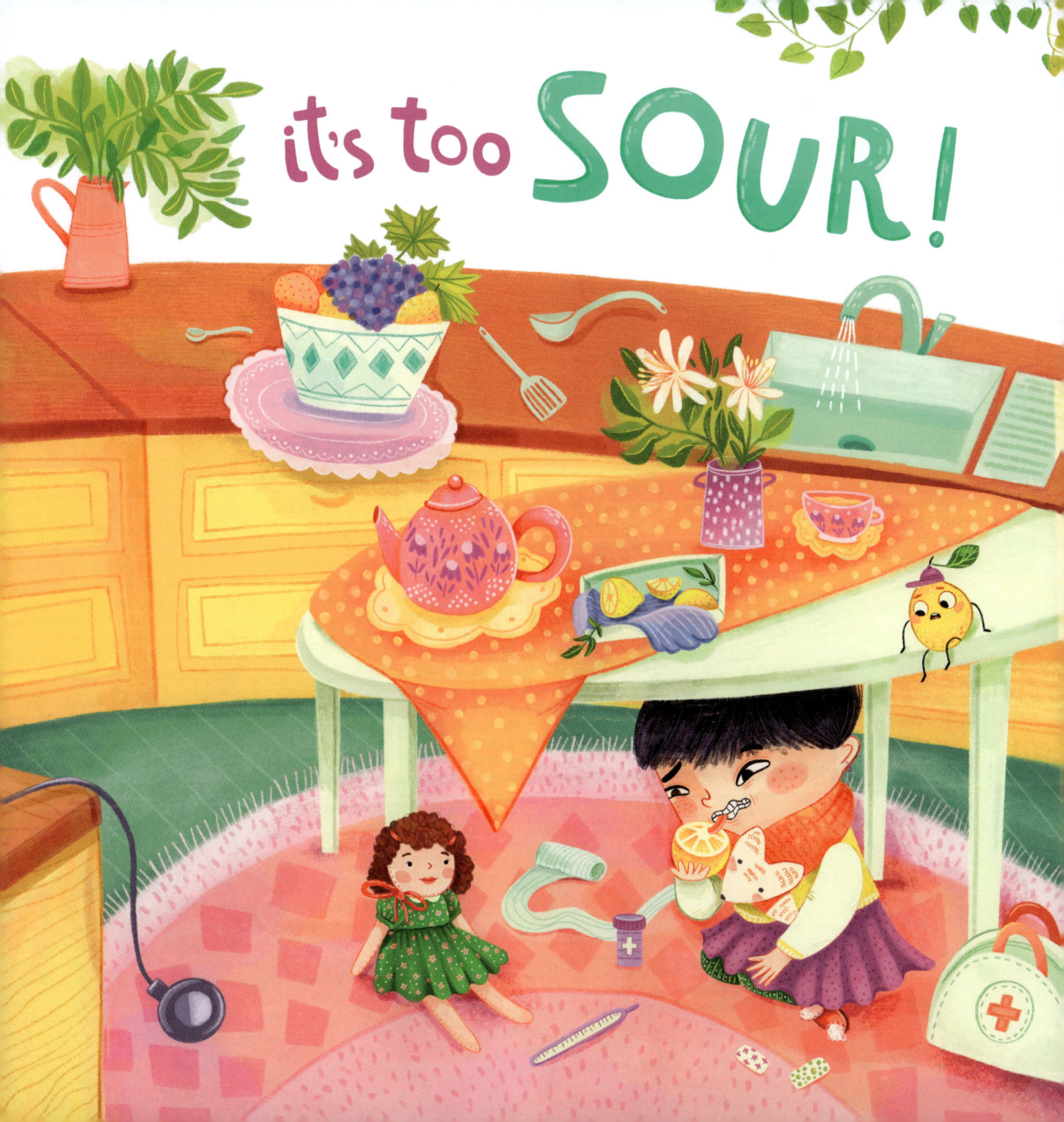

it's too Bumpy!

it's too SMELLY!

And it always **squirts** when I squeeze it!

When I am a Doctor,

I will make LEMONS SOFT AND FLUFFY!

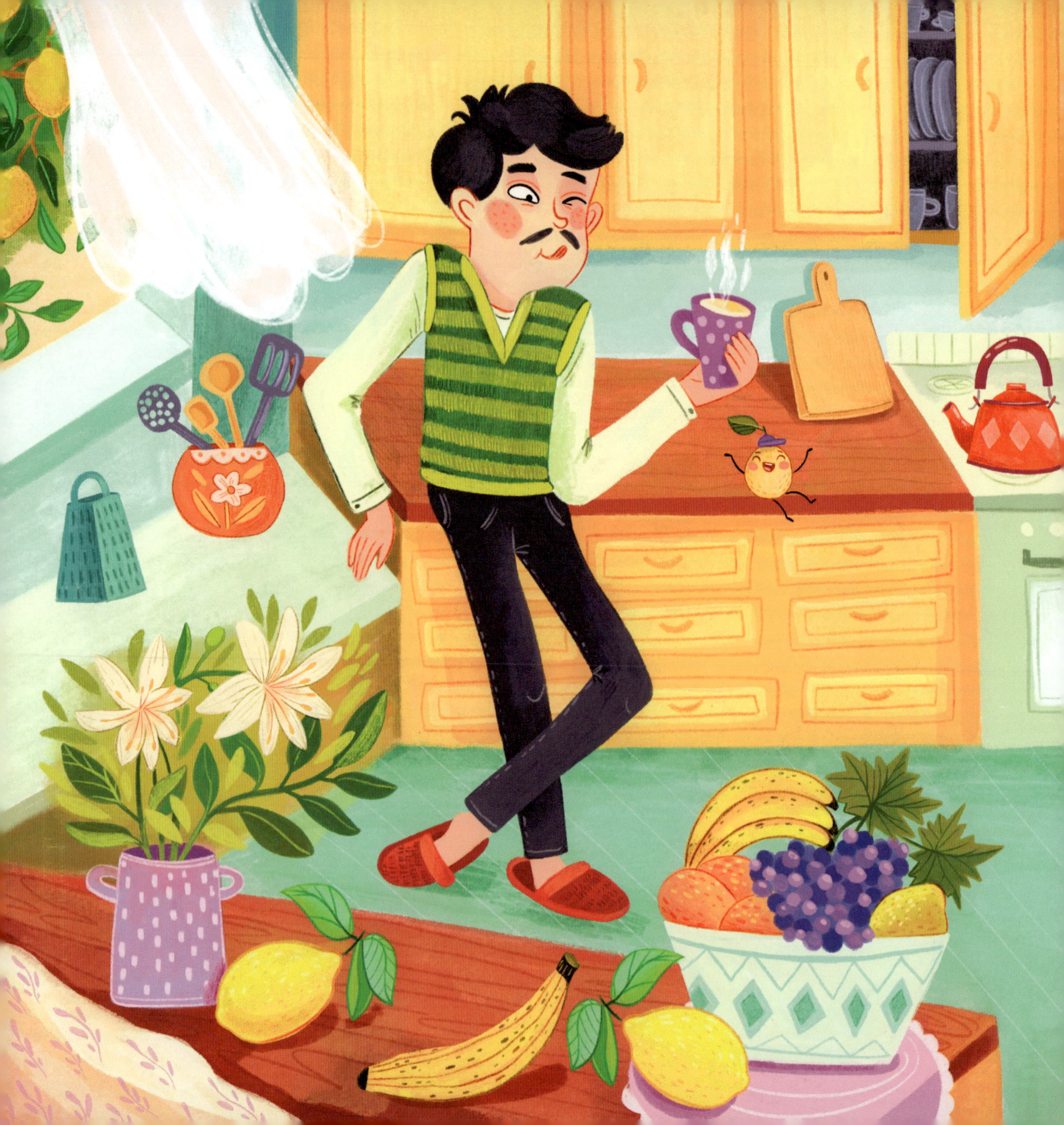

My daddy says he DOES NOT LIKE LEMON either, but he LOVES this yummy DRINK

It is the COLOUR of a FLUFFY CHICK

It is WARM like a HUG

It is made of SMALL frozen HEARTS

It has got SWEET HONEY in it

AND it is super-duper DELICIOUS!

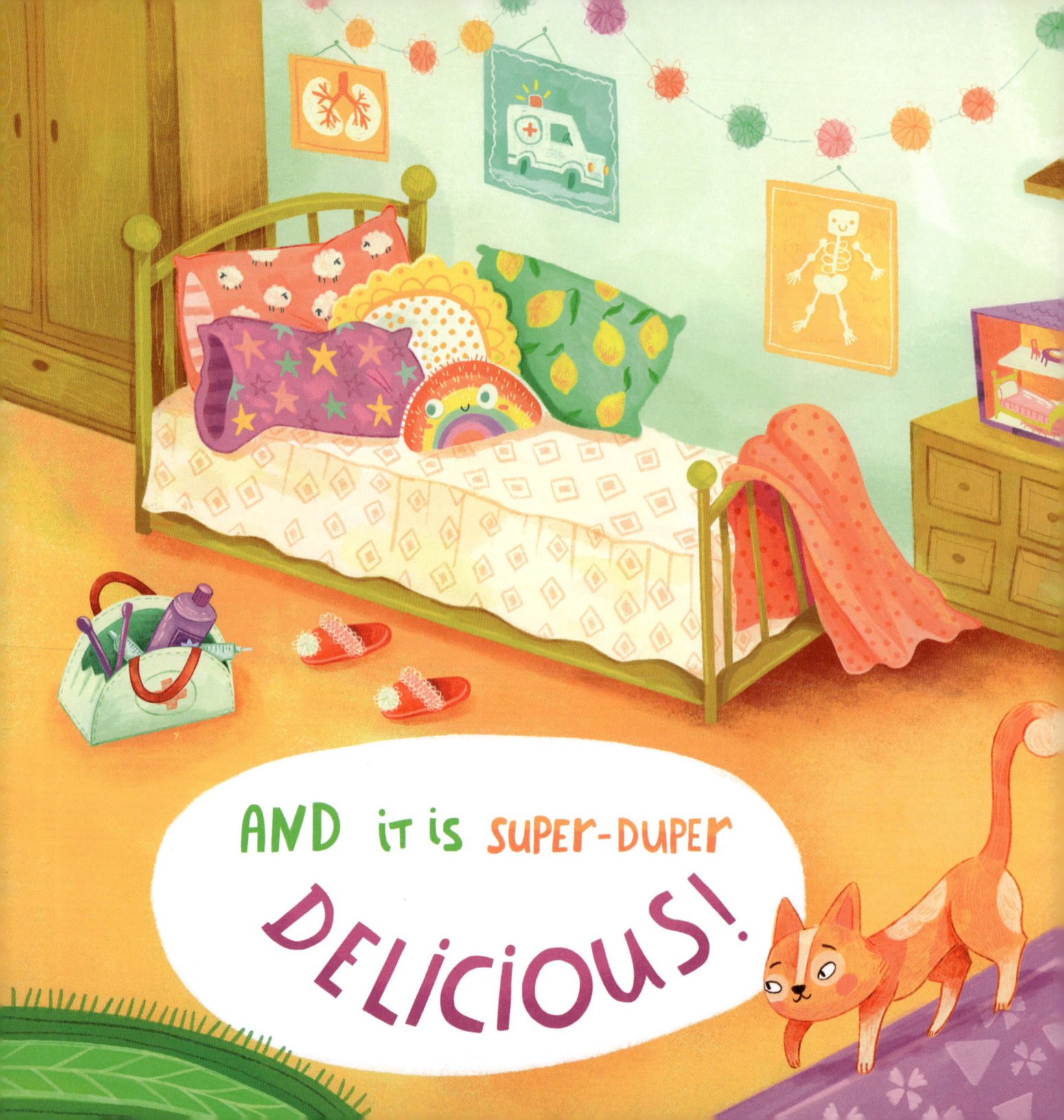

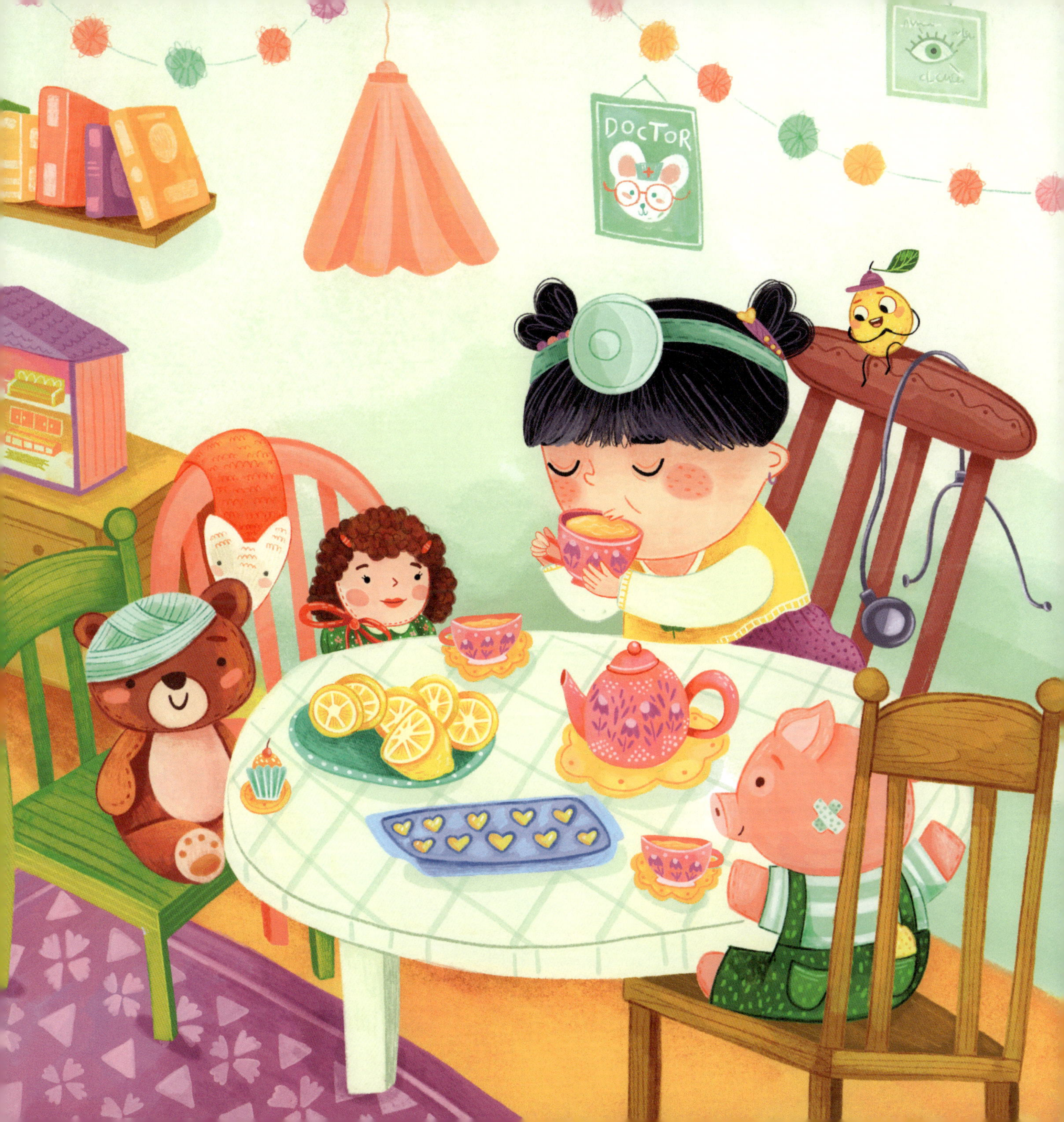
DOCTOR

HONEY & LEMON HEARTS

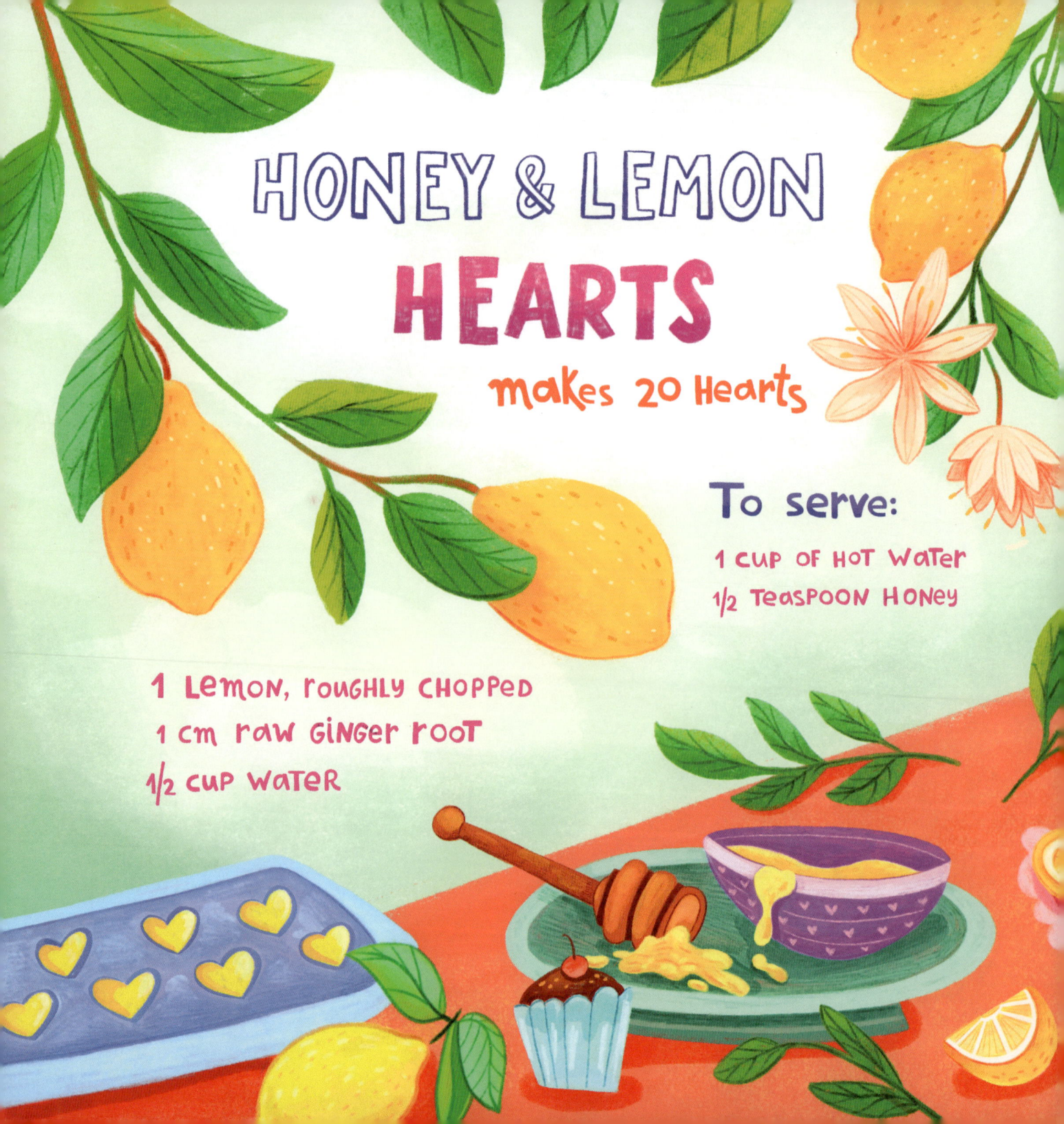

makes 20 Hearts

To serve:
1 cup of hot water
1/2 teaspoon honey

1 lemon, roughly chopped
1 cm raw ginger root
1/2 cup water

Method

- Add all the ingredients into a blender and blend until they form a paste.
- Transfer the mixture into a silicone ice cube tray and freeze for 2-3 hours.
- Add 1 cube into a cup of hot water. Stir it then add honey!

No Bake Lemon Truffles

Makes 20 Truffles

1 cup ground almonds
1/3 cup desiccated coconut
1/4 cup maple syrup
1 tablespoon coconut oil
1 teaspoon lemon juice
Zest of 2 lemons

Chocolate Coating

100g white chocolate
1 tablespoon coconut oil

Method:

- Add all the ingredients into a food processor and blend until they form a paste.
- Roll the mixture into small balls and set aside.
- Combine chocolate and coconut oil in a small bowl and microwave for 60 seconds. Stir well melted ingredients.
- Using a spoon, dip lemon balls into the chocolate mixture. Place chocolate balls onto a tray lined with baking paper and freeze for 10 minutes.
- Enjoy immediately or keep in a freezer and enjoy later!

No Bake Lemon & Blueberries Flapjacks

Makes 20 bars

- 3 tablespoons lemon zest, grated
- 1 tablespoon lemon juice
- 1/2 cup mixed raw or roasted nuts
- 1 cup oats
- 1/4 cup coconut oil
- 1/4 cup peanut butter
- 1/4 cup maple syrup
- 1 tablespoon cinnamon
- 1/4 cup dried blueberries

Optional Chocolate Coating

- 50g white chocolate
- 1 teaspoon coconut oil
- 1 tablespoon lemon zest, grated

Method:

- Add all the ingredients apart from blueberries, into a food processor and mix for 30 seconds.
- Transfer the mixture into a loaf tin lined with baking paper, add blueberries and smooth with a spoon.
- If making the chocolate coating, combine chocolate with coconut oil and microwave for 30 seconds then pour over the flapjack mixture. Sprinkle with lemon zest.
- Move flapjacks into a freezer for 30 minutes until the mixture is solid. Remove from the freezer and cut into bars.
- Enjoy!

Other Books From the I Will Never Ever Eat the Rainbow Series

I Will Never Ever Eat Avocado
ANA BALL

I Will Never Ever Eat Beetroot
ANA BALL

I Will Never Ever Eat Carrot
ANA BALL

I Will Never Ever Eat Lemon
ANA BALL

LEMON

LEMON

Printed in Dunstable, United Kingdom